Cooking in the Wok

Fish

© Naumann & Göbel Verlagsgesellschaft mbH, a subsidiary of
VEMAG Verlags- und Medien Aktiengesellschaft, Cologne
www.apollo-intermedia.de

Complete production: Naumann & Göbel Verlagsgesellschaft mbH, Cologne
Printed in Germany

ISBN 3-625-11238-8

Cooking in the Wok

Fish

NAUMANN & GÖBEL

Contents

Introduction

Wok with Fish

The world-wide success of cooking in the wok is due to a style of cookery that is both simple and convincing: fresh ingredients, short cooking times and aromatic spices. If these principles are paired with fine fish and exquisite seafood, cooking turns into a culinary event. The countries of Asia are surrounded by the ocean, which explains why fish and seafood traditionally play a major role in Asian cooking. What's more, when cooking fish in a wok, the principles of Asian cuisine unfold to perfection: the ingredients are cooked most gently and the flavour is harmoniously balanced.

Preparation

All kinds of fresh- and saltwater fish are suitable for preparing in the wok, as well as mussels and shells, prawns, lobsters and crabs, and especially squid. The fish is usually cut into bite-sized chunks before cooking, but it can also be fried whole. There is a trick to make sure that squid, the flesh of which sometimes has a tendency to be a bit tough, becomes tender: slice open the tubes, lay them on the work surface with the inside downwards and make diamond-shaped incisions into the outer side, using a very sharp knife. During the cooking process, the squid chunks then rise up in that shape, which also looks very decorative.

Prawns and shrimps can be found in many varieties in every ocean around the globe. In Asian cooking, the large tiger and king prawns are predominantly used, as they can be found in the sub-tropic waters of the Indian and Pacific Oceans. The shell of a prawn is loosened from its bottom side. Make an incision into the back with a knife in order to remove the black bowels.

When cooking mussels and shells, their freshness is vital. They have to close up while you are soaking them in cold water. The ones that remain open have to be discarded. Once they are cooked, they should have opened; this time, the ones that remain closed must not be eaten, but discarded.

Scallops have wonderfully tender flesh. It is best to buy them in the shell and then open them yourself. Hold the shell tightly with the flat side pointing upwards, then carefully drive a knife in between the upper and lower side of

the shell and cut through the muscle. Now you can pull off the grey coat and discard it; the red roe is loosened and also used for cooking.

If you marinate the fish before cooking it, it will turn out especially aromatic. Recommendable for marinating are all kinds of Asian sauces such as fish, oyster, soy or hoisin sauce, but rice wine is also very suitable for marinating. Exotic herbs and spices give the marinade its special flair – and these explain the unusual attraction of Asian cooking.

When fish dishes are combined with vegetables, start by cooking the vegetables, as most vegetables have a longer cooking time than fish. This way, you prevent the fish from flaking. In general, fish and seafood are both suitable for pungent spices and for sweet and sour flavours and go well with vegetables or with exotic fruits such as pineapple or mango. Fish dishes are best accompanied with fragrant or wild rice.

The Wok

The traditional wok is made of cast iron and has the shape of a half-globe. Both the material and the shape help to spread the heat evenly and quickly, from the round base to the upper rim. This cooking device is versatile and extremely economic; its career began more than 3000 years ago in China. The pan (wok is the Cantonese term for pan) was developed when it became necessary to quickly prepare food over one single flame, at a time when timber was scarce in the country. The invention proved successful and the wok made its triumphal march through all of Asia and in the meantime also through Europe.

Modern woks have been adapted to electric and gas ovens and often come with a flat base. A wok can be had in several sizes and also made of various materials such as high-grade steel, aluminium or copper. When choosing a pan with a coating, make sure to only use tools that will not scratch the surface. A wok should lie well in your hand. There are some models with two handles and some with one long handle.

8

Cooking Methods

The wok is a versatile talent. Meat, fish and vegetables can be prepared in the most varying ways.

The classic mode of cooking in the wok is stir-frying. Depending on the required cooking time, the various ingredients are given into very little, extremely hot oil one at a time and are then tossed and stirred continually. Once an ingredient is cooked, it is pushed up towards the rim of the wok, and then the next ingredient is added to the centre of the pan. This method ensures that every ingredient is cooked to perfection. Since cooking in the wok is very fast, the ingredients have to be ready to use: rinsed, trimmed and chopped.

When braising, the ingredients are gently fried in small amounts and then some liquid such as stock is added. Firmly cover the wok and leave the ingredients to simmer.

Meat, fish or vegetables can also be wrapped in rice leaves or coated with a batter, the so-called tempura, and then deep fat fried until they are golden brown. The wok is very suitable for deep fat frying because you will need much less fat than with the customary methods. In order to find out whether the oil has reached the ideal temperature, dip a wooden skewer into the oil. If you see small bubbles gather around the skewer, the oil is hot enough.

Steaming is a very gentle and healthy method of cooking with a long tradition in China. The ingredients are placed into special bamboo baskets which have been soaked in water beforehand and are then cooked in the covered wok, with very little liquid. It is important that the wok is firmly closed and that the cooking liquid does not touch the baskets. During the steaming process, you should check regularly to ensure that there is enough liquid in the wok.

The large variety of Asian spices, herbs and ingredients only seems confusing at first sight. Since cooking in the wok has become trendy, many supermarkets have adapted their range accordingly. The less-known ingredients can be bought in Asian specialist shops.

Alfalfa sprouts
are procured from a forage plant that is also known as lucerne.

Bonito flakes
are made of dried saltwater fish, preferably tuna.

Cardamom
has a flavour reminiscent of cloves and cinnamon.

Chillies
are the pods of the chilli pepper plant. Depending on their colour – green, yellow or red – their taste can be very pungent to mild. Another rule of thumb: the smaller the spicier.

Chinese chives
also called Cuchai chives. These chives smell a bit like European chives, but their taste is more like that of garlic.

Coriander
also known as Chinese parsley. In Asian cooking, the whole plant is used, the aromatic leaves as well as the seeds, which are the size of peppercorns, can be used whole or ground, and taste of cinnamon and nutmeg.

Cumin
seeds look like caraway seeds, but the flavour is very different. If you are interested to know what cumin tastes like, try a bitter liqueur: this is where it is used in Western tradition.

Curry
powder is a blend of spices that can vary from one country to another. When making curry, the following ingredients may be used: cardamom, cumin, turmeric, pepper, cinnamon, cloves, chillies and nutmeg.

Five spice powder
Depending on the country, the mixture can vary but it is always based on fennel seeds, cloves, cardamom or pepper, star anise and cinnamon.

Galangal root
belongs to the ginger family and is similar in flavour, though less spicy.

Garam masala
is a typical Indian spice blend composed of various spices.

Ghee
is Indian lard used for baking and cooking and made of clarified butter.

Ginger
is the favourite spice in Asian cooking. These bizarrely formed roots with their yellow-brown colour can taste anything from aromatic to spicy. Ginger is known to tone up the digestive system and also has bactericidal agents.

Hoisin sauce
is a rather sweet, brown seasoning sauce which is made out of soy beans, chillies, garlic and spices.

Kaffir lime
The finely chopped leaves or rind of this plant are used for their lemony flavour.

Lemon grass
is a perennial, very aromatic grass. The stalks have a fine lemony aroma.

Mirin
is the slightly sweet Japanese rice wine, comparable to our sherry.

Miso
is a seasoning paste made of rice, soy or mung bean sprouts and sometimes barley and is offered in many different versions.

Nam prik
is the Burmese version of sambal. This paste consists mainly of chillies, garlic, shallots and a shrimp or prawn paste.

Oyster sauce
is a brown, thick seasoning sauce. It is rather salty and should only be used sparingly.

Palm sugar
is made of palm trees and used to season both sweet and salty dishes.

Rau om
is a herbacious perennial; the leaves are aromatic, rather sweet and taste of cumin. Rau Om is very popular in Thai and Vietnamese cooking.

Sambal oelek
is a devilishly hot spice paste made of chillies. Anyone who has ever tasted it will certainly not forget it.

Spring onions
look like leeks and are milder than their round sisters, the large or small onions.

Tamarind
is an Indian date that tastes slightly sour and is used for making sauce, paste or purée.

Tandoori paste
is a hot Indian curry paste. There is also a herb mixture referred to as tandoori.

Tempura flour
is an especially fine flour type used for the typical dishes prepared by deep fat frying.

Thai basil
has hardly anything in common with the basil we know in Europe. Its leaves are less fine and the taste reminds one slightly of aniseed.

Tom yum goong paste
is a paste made of many different ingredients, the most prominent of which are lemon grass, onions, fish and prawns.

Turmeric
also known as Indian saffron, gives the curry its typical yellow colour. Turmeric tastes mildly of pepper and slightly bitter.

Wan tan leaves
are very thin leaves made of rice flour.

Recipes with Fish

Be it deep fat fried, fried, braised or steamed, cooking in the wok holds many fascinating variations in store for lovers of fine fish cuisine. Discover the whole palette of Far Eastern fish specialities, from monkfish to squid.

Sweet and Sour Gilthead with Leek and Carrot Strips

Serves 4

4 gilthead fillets,
with their skin
(120 g/4.5 oz each)

6 medium-sized carrots

4 leeks

4 tbsp vegetable oil

2 tbsp tomato ketchup

4 tbsp sweet and sour
sauce

2 tbsp fish sauce

2 sprigs coriander

Preparation time

approx. 25 minutes

Per serving

approx. 347 kcal/1 455 kj

31 g P

16 g F

15 g C

1 Rinse and pat dry the fish fillets and remove the fish bones. Then cut them into 3 cm/1.2 in chunks. Rinse and peel the carrots and cut them into fine strips using the slicer. Cut the leeks into sticks of approx. 15 cm/6 in, rinse and shake dry.

2 Briefly fry the fish chunks in the wok in 2 tablespoons sizzling oil, only with the skin side down, then remove.

3 Stir-fry the vegetables in the remaining oil, let them wilt, then season with ketchup and sweet and sour sauce; pour the fish sauce over.

4 Now return the fish chunks and gently fold them in. Towards the end, add the finely chopped coriander. Be careful that the sauce does not thicken too much – if need be, add some water.

16

Salmon Trout with Chicory and Fried Chillies

Serves 4

500 g/17 oz
salmon trout fillet

6 chicory

5 large, dried green chillies

2 sticks lemon grass

6 tbsp vegetable oil

6 tbsp oyster sauce

1/2 bunch Thai basil

Preparation time

approx. 20 minutes

Per serving

approx. 306 kcal/1 282 kj

27 g P

19 g F

3 g C

1 Rinse the salmon trout fillet, pat dry well and cut into 3 cm/1.2 in chunks. Coarsely chop the chicory and remove the stalk. Crumble up the chillies. Finely slice the lemon grass sticks.

2 Heat the oil in the wok, gently fry the chillies and then remove.

3 Stir-fry the chicory in the same oil over a high heat, then add the oyster sauce.

4 Now add the fish chunks, sliced lemon grass and fried chillies and stir carefully. Add the plucked basil leaves towards the end.

18

Fried Rice Noodles with Squid and Bitter Gourds

Serves 4

250 g/9 oz rice noodles

500 g/17 oz squid

1 bunch coriander

4 tbsp vegetable oil

2 bitter gourds

2 dried red chillies

4 tbsp oyster sauce

1 tsp sambal oelek

Preparation time

approx. 30 minutes

Per serving

approx. 368 kcal/1 536 kj

33 g P

13 g F

33 g C

1 Cook the noodles according to the instructions on the package and drain them in a colander.

2 Trim and thoroughly wash the squid tubes, slice them open, lay them with the skin side downwards, cut a fine rhombus-pattern into the back and then cut them into chunks. Rinse and dry the bitter gourds, seed and cut into 1 cm/0.4 in slices. Chop the coriander leaves into 1 cm/0.4 in slices.

3 Heat the oil in the wok, coarsely crush the chillies and stir-fry in the oil. Add the squid chunks, briefly stir-fry and then add the oyster sauce and remove.

4 Now put the sliced bitter gourds into the wok, add approx. 100 ml/3 fl oz water and braise briefly.

5 Give the squid chunks and chillies back into the wok, add the cooked rice noodles, season with sambal oelek, stir in the sliced coriander, toss and serve.

Fried Perch with Red Curry and Lychees

Serves 4

500 g/17 oz
skinless perch

2 tbsp oyster sauce

4 tbsp fish sauce

1 bitter gourd

1 dried large chilli

4 tbsp vegetable oil

1 tbsp palm sugar

1 tbsp red curry paste

2 tins unsweetened
coconut milk
(400 ml/14 fl oz each)

1 tin lychees
(400 ml/14 fl oz)

Preparation time

approx. 15 minutes

(plus 30 minutes
for marinating)

Per serving

approx. 318 kcal/1 332 kj

25 g P

13 g F

24 g C

1 Rinse and pat dry the perch fillet and cut into 3 cm/1.2 in chunks. Marinate in the fish and oyster sauces for 30 minutes.

2 Halve and seed the bitter gourd and cut into slices 0.5 cm/0.2 in thick. Cut the chilli into rings.

3 Heat the oil in the wok, gently fry the finely chopped palm sugar and curry paste, then add the coconut milk and bring to the boil. Add the bitter gourds and leave to simmer gently for 5 minutes.

4 Add the drained lychees and the fish chunks and leave to draw for 2 minutes more. Towards the end, sprinkle with chilli rings.

Gilthead with Peanut Sauce and Green Peppercorns

Serves 4

150 g/5 oz
unsalted peanuts

1 tbsp red curry paste

1 tbsp palm sugar

1 tin coconut milk
(400 ml/14 fl oz)

3 tbsp fish sauce

700 g/1 lb 8 oz gilthead

1–2 tbsp tempura flour

6 tbsp sunflower oil

200 g/7 oz broccoli

150 g/5 oz
oyster mushrooms

2 strings fresh green
peppercorns

3 tbsp oyster sauce

2 tbsp fish sauce

Preparation time

approx. 40 minutes

Per serving

approx. 643 kcal/2 691 kj
48 g P
41 g F
14 g C

1   Roast the peanuts in the wok without any fat until they are golden brown, then leave to cool and finely grind them in your blender.

2   Bring the curry paste, palm sugar, 100 ml/3 fl oz coconut milk and 100 ml/3fl oz water to the boil stirring continually. Season with fish sauce. Add the peanuts and the remaining coconut milk, leave to simmer gently for approx. 15 minutes, stirring now and then.

3   Rinse and pat dry the gilthead and make diagonal incisions on both sides, starting from the head and down along the main bone, with a distance of 0.5 cm/0.2 in between each incision. Coat the gilthead on both sides with tempura flour and fry in 3 tablespoons oil for approx. 8 minutes, until it has turned golden brown.

4   Rinse the broccoli and break up into florets, peel the stalk and cut into slices. Trim the oyster mushrooms and cut into halves or thirds, depending on the size.

5   Heat the remaining oil in the wok. One after the other, stir-fry broccoli, mushrooms and peppercorns loosened from the strings over a high heat and then season with the oyster and fish sauces. Arrange the fish on the vegetables and serve with the peanut sauce.

Salmon with Button Mushrooms and Spinach

Serves 4

500 g/17 oz salmon fillet

4 tbsp fish sauce

200 g/7 oz
button mushrooms

400 g/14 oz
fresh leaf spinach

2 tbsp vegetable oil

2 tbsp sesame oil

1 tbsp sesame seeds

1 tsp sambal oelek

Preparation time

approx. 30 minutes

(plus 10 minutes
for marinating)

Per serving

approx. 480 kcal/2 012 kj

30 g P

37 g F

1 g C

1 Rinse and pat dry the salmon and cut into strips. Marinate in the fish sauce for approx. 10 minutes. Trim and slice the button mushrooms. Wash and shake dry the spinach, then trim it.

2 Heat the vegetable and sesame oils in the wok, briefly stir-fry the button mushrooms, then add the spinach and let it wilt.

3 Push the vegetables to the rim of the wok and add the salmon strips to the centre. Sprinkle with sesame seeds and fry carefully. When turning the fish over be careful that it does not flake.

4 Towards the end, carefully fold the vegetables in with the fish and season with sambal oelek.

26

Monkfish in Black Bean Sauce with Long Beans

Serves 4

800 g/1 lb 12 oz
monkfish

1 garlic clove

2 tbsp black bean sauce

300 g/10 oz shallots

400 g/14 oz long beans

4 tbsp vegetable oil

2 tbsp oyster sauce

1 tbsp chilli garlic sauce

1/2 bunch Thai basil

Preparation time

approx. 25 minutes

(plus 10 minutes
for marinating)

Per serving

approx. 335 kcal/1 402 kj

40 g P

14 g F

9 g C

1 Rinse and pat dry the monkfish and cut into chunks. Peel and finely chop the garlic clove and marinate the fish for approx. 10 minutes in the garlic and black bean sauce.

2 Peel the shallots, rinse and trim the long beans and cut into 8 cm/3.2 in pieces.

3 Heat 3 tablespoons oil in the wok and first fry the shallots until they turn golden brown, then add the long beans, fry, pour oyster and chilli garlic sauces over, toss and remove.

4 Now give the monkfish into the wok and fry for 3–5 minutes. Return the vegetables, stir in the chopped Thai basil and serve.

28

Fish Balls in Vermicelli Batter

Serves 4

400 g/14 oz pike fillet

80 g/2.75 oz
shelled crabmeat

Juice of 1 lemon

Salt

Freshly ground white
pepper

2 shallots

3 raw eggs

2 tbsp Thai basil

50 g/1.75 oz vermicelli

2 tbsp oil for deep
fat frying

4 tbsp sweet and sour
sauce

Preparation time

approx. 20 minutes

Per serving

approx. 329 kcal/1 378 kj

21 g P

19 g F

16 g C

1 Rinse and pat dry the pike fillet and cut into small cubes. Also cube the crabmeat. You can also chop them in your blender. Season with lemon juice, salt and pepper. Add the chopped shallots, 1 egg and the minced Thai basil and mix well. Season again with salt and pepper.

2 Break the vermicelli into small pieces or cut them with your scissors.

3 Form the fish paste into small balls, using two teaspoons. First dip into the remaining, whisked eggs, then roll in the vermicelli.

4 Deep fat fry in sizzling oil in the wok and then drain on some absorbent kitchen paper. Serve with sweet and sour sauce as a dip.

Salmon with Baby Sweet Corn and Chinese Chives

Serves 4

20 baby sweet corns
6 tbsp sunflower oil
1 tbsp oyster sauce
4 slices salmon
2 tbsp tempura flour
1 bunch Chinese chives
3 tbsp tamarind purée
2 tbsp fish sauce

Preparation time

approx. 25 minutes

Per serving

approx. 595 kcal/2 493 kj
42 g P
35 g F
19 g C

1 Rinse and dry the baby sweet corns, halve lengthwise and stir-fry in the wok in 1 tablespoon sizzling oil. Add the oyster sauce and remove.

2 Rinse and pat dry the salmon and cut into largish chunks. Coat with tempura flour and fry in 3 tablespoons oil, until crispy golden. Drain on absorbent kitchen paper and keep warm.

3 Rinse and dry the Chinese chives, cut into 5 cm/2 in sticks and equally stir-fry in a little oil. Add the baby sweet corn and season with tamarind purée and fish sauce, leave to simmer for 3 minutes.

4 Add the salmon chunks towards the end and carefully fold in.

Tuna Chunks in a Sesame Coat with Radish and Green Asparagus

Serves 4

500 g/17 oz tuna

2 tbsp fish sauce

4 tbsp sesame seeds

1 bunch green asparagus

400 g/14 oz white radish

4 tbsp vegetable oil

1 tbsp sesame oil

1/2 tsp palm sugar

6 tbsp oyster sauce

Preparation time

approx. 25 minutes

Per serving

approx. 544 kcal/2 280 kj

33 g P

41 g F

6 g C

1 Rinse and pat dry the tuna and cut into 3 cm/1.2 in chunks, then sprinkle with fish sauce and coat with sesame seeds.

2 Rinse and dry the asparagus and cut into finger-sized pieces. Rinse and dry the radish and cut into 4 cm/1.6 in sticks.

3 Heat 2 tablespoons vegetable oil and the sesame oil in the wok and briefly stir-fry the asparagus, then add the radish sticks and sprinkle with the grated palm sugar. Remove.

4 Heat the remaining oil, give in the tuna chunks one by one and carefully fry on both sides. Towards the end, return the vegetables into the wok, pour the oyster sauce over, stir carefully and serve immediately.

Braised Squid

Serves 4

2 tbsp rice vinegar

3 tbsp soy sauce

1/2 tsp caster sugar

1 tbsp peanut oil

500 g/17 oz
frozen squid rings

1 tbsp oil

Garlic mustard
for sprinkling

Preparation time

approx. 25 minutes

Per serving

approx. 176 kcal/736 kj

23 g P

6 g F

2 g C

1 Mix the vinegar with soy sauce, caster sugar and oil.

2 Pour the squid rings into a colander and leave to thaw.

3 Heat the oil and briefly stir-fry the squid rings over a high heat.

4 Add the sauce, bring to the boil and then braise the squids for approx. 10 minutes.

5 Rinse and shake dry the garlic mustard and cut into fine rings.

6 Serve the squid sprinkled with the herbs.

Whole-grain Rice with Salmon and Spicy Bean Sauce

Serves 4

250 g/9 oz
whole-grain rice

400 g/14 oz salmon fillet

2 tbsp spicy bean sauce

200 g/7 oz
cherry tomatoes

4 tbsp vegetable oil

1/2 bunch coriander

Preparation time

approx. 30 minutes

(plus 10 minutes
for marinating)

Per serving

approx. 462 kcal/1 933 kj

24 g P

24 g F

32 g C

1 Cook the whole-grain rice according to the instructions on the package and set aside.

2 Rinse and pat dry the salmon and cut into 3 cm/1.2 in chunks, then marinate for approx. 10 minutes in the spicy bean sauce. Rinse, dry and halve the cherry tomatoes.

3 Heat the oil in the wok, briefly stir-fry the salmon chunks, then add the halved tomatoes, the fish sauce and the cooked rice. Turn carefully and fry until the salmon is tender.

4 Rinse and shake dry the coriander and pluck off the leaves. Sprinkle over the rice just before serving.

Fried Monkfish with Shiitake and Bamboo Shoots

Serves 4

650 g/1 lb 7 oz
skinless monkfish fillet

100 g/3.5 oz
shiitake mushrooms

1 bunch spring onions

2 garlic cloves

2 green chillies

200 g/7 oz bamboo
shoots (in a jar)

4 tbsp sunflower oil

3 tbsp oyster sauce

2 tbsp fish sauce

Preparation time

approx. 25 minutes

Per serving

approx. 269 kcal/1 126 kj

33 g P

11 g F

6 g C

1 Rinse and pat dry the monkfish and cut into 2 cm/0.8 in chunks. Trim the shiitake mushrooms and halve, depending on their size. Rinse, dry and trim the spring onions and cut into 2 cm/0.8 in diagonal slices. Peel the garlic cloves and finely chop them with the chillies. Slice the bamboo shoots.

2 Fry the monkfish in the wok, using half the oil, until it is crispy brown on both sides. Remove and set aside.

3 One after the other, stir-fry the spring onions, mushrooms, garlic, chilli and sliced bamboo shoots in the remaining sizzling oil. Season with the oyster and fish sauces.

4 Towards the end, carefully fold in the fish, heat up again and serve.

Cod Curry with Tomatoes and Pineapple

Serves 4

200 g/7 oz tomatoes

1/4 pineapple

100 g/3.5 oz
baby sweet corn

4 Kaffir lime leaves

600 g/1 lb 5 oz cod fillet

1 tbsp yellow curry paste

2 tbsp palm sugar

1 tin coconut milk
(400 g/14 fl oz)

3 tbsp fish sauce

3 sprigs Thai basil

Preparation time

approx. 25 minutes

Per serving

approx. 230 kcal/965 kj

29 g P

2 g F

23 g C

1 Rinse and dry the cherry tomatoes. Peel the pineapple, remove the stalk and cut the flesh into cubes. Rinse, dry and coarsely chop the baby sweet corn; finely slice the Kaffir lime leaves. Rinse and pat dry the cod fillet and cut into bite-sized chunks.

2 Mix the curry paste with grated palm sugar and 100 ml/3 fl oz coconut milk until it is smooth, then bring to the boil in the wok, stirring continually.

3 Pour in the remaining coconut milk and season with fish sauce. Give the fish chunks, tomatoes, baby sweet corn and pineapple to the curry and briefly leave to draw.

4 Stir in the Kaffir lime leaves and plucked basil leaves and season once again with fish sauce.

Steamed Lotus Root with Salmon and Red Chillies

Serves 4

400 g/14 oz salmon

1 bunch spring onions

1 tin cooked lotus root
(400 g/14 oz)

6 tbsp fish sauce

1 tbsp roasted
sesame oil

1 handful red chillies

Rice vinegar and coriander
leaves for dipping

Preparation time

approx. 35 minutes

Per serving

approx. 276 kcal/1 154 kj

24 g P

18 g F

3 g C

1 Rinse and pat dry the salmon and cut into slices. Trim and rinse the spring onions and cut into fine rings.

2 Make alternating layers of lotus root and salmon: place a slice of lotus root onto a slice of salmon, sprinkle with fish sauce and sesame oil. Continue until all ingredients have been used up. A slice of lotus root should be on top of each of these little tarts.

3 Place the tarts into two largish bamboo baskets. Lay the chillies between the tarts and sprinkle spring onion rings over them.

4 Place the bamboo baskets, one on top of the other, into the wok, fill some water into the wok, firmly close the lid and steam for approx. 15 minutes. Change the baskets after half of the steaming time to ensure that both are steamed evenly. This dish goes well with a dip made of rice vinegar and coriander leaves.

Scorpionfish with Baby Sweet Corn, Snow Peas and Mint

Serves 4

4 scorpionfish fillets
(150 g/3.5 oz each)

3 tbsp fish sauce

200 g/7 oz snow peas

200 g/7 oz
baby sweet corn

2 carrots

6 tbsp vegetable oil

1 tbsp shrimp paste

3 tbsp oyster sauce

1 tsp sambal oelek

5 sprigs mint

Preparation time

approx. 15 minutes
(plus 30 minutes
for marinating)

Per serving

approx. 391 kcal/1 637 kj
32 g P
19 g F
19 g C

1 Rinse the scorpionfish fillets and thoroughly pat dry. Cut the fish into 3 cm/1.2 in chunks and marinate approx. 30 minutes in the fish sauce, leaving the skin on.

2 Rinse and dry the snow peas and baby sweet corn and halve diagonally. Rinse, trim, peel and halve the carrots and cut into strips.

3 Heat 4 tablespoons oil in the wok and stir-fry the vegetables, then add the shrimp paste, oyster sauce and sambal oelek and pour in 200 ml/7 fl oz water. Remove.

4 Stir-fry the fish in the remaining oil, then return the vegetables and carefully stir. Towards the end, sprinkle with plucked mint leaves.

Serves 4

800 g/1 lb 12 oz
pikeperch fillet
2 tbsp fish sauce
120 g/4 oz aubergines
1 tbsp red curry paste
1 tin coconut milk
(400 ml/14 fl oz)
1 tbsp palm sugar
200 g/7 oz
water chestnuts
2 Kaffir lime leaves

Preparation time

approx. 30 minutes
(plus 10 minutes
for marinating)

Per serving

approx. 315 kcal/1 320 kj
47 g P
3 g F
25 g C

1 Rinse and pat dry the pikeperch, cut into bite-sized chunks and marinate in some fish sauce for 10 minutes. Rinse and dry the aubergines and cut into cubes.

2 Mix the curry paste with 200 ml/7 fl oz coconut milk, 100 ml/3 fl oz water and grated palm sugar and bring to the boil, stirring continually. Add the remaining coconut milk and the aubergine cubes and leave to simmer gently for approx. 10 minutes. Season with the fish sauce.

3 Add the well-drained water chestnuts. Now add the fish chunks and briefly cook until tender.

4 Finely slice the Kaffir lime leaves, stir into the dish and serve in small bowls.

Squid with Fried Broccoli and Button Mushrooms

Serves 4

4 medium-sized
squid tubes

800 g/1 lb 12 oz broccoli

120 g/4 oz
button mushrooms

2 garlic cloves

2–3 tbsp sunflower oil

2 tbsp oyster sauce

2 tbsp fish sauce

1/2 tsp ground coriander
seeds

Caster sugar

Preparation time

approx. 25 minutes

Per serving

approx. 225 kcal/943 kj

26 g P

9 g F

7 g C

1 Thoroughly wash and then pat dry the squid tubes. Slice them open on one side and spread them out on the work surface, the inside showing up. Take a sharp knife and cut rhombus-shaped incisions into it, with a distance of approx. 1 cm. Then cut the squids into 5 cm/2 in chunks.

2 Rinse and trim the broccoli and break up into florets; peel and slice the stalk. Trim the button mushrooms, rub them with kitchen paper and cut into quarters. Peel and finely chop the garlic cloves.

3 Thoroughly heat the oil in the wok and stir-fry the squid chunks for 2 minutes. Remove, then fry the garlic, broccoli and button mushrooms.

4 Towards the end, return the squid chunks and season the lot with the oyster and fish sauces, coriander and a pinch of caster sugar.

50

Red Snapper
in Yoghurt Sauce

Serves 4

4 red snappers,
ready for cooking

Salt

1/2 tsp turmeric

4 onions

1 knob grated root ginger
(approx. 5 cm/2 in)

4 seeded green chillies

1/2 tsp cumin

3–4 dried red chillies

300 g/10 oz plain yoghurt

1/2 tsp caster sugar

Oil for frying

3 cloves

2 cardamom pods

2.5 cm/1.5 in
cinnamon stick

3 bay leaves

Preparation time

approx. 30 minutes

(plus 1 hour minimum
drawing time)

Per serving

approx. 298 kcal/1 250 kj

48 g P

8 g F

7 g C

1. Rub the fish on the inside and outside with salt and turmeric and leave to draw at room temperature for at least 1 hour.

2. Peel and coarsely chop the onions, then blend them with ginger and green chillies to make a smooth paste. Give this paste through a sieve and squash out the juice with a spoon. Keep the remains and the juice.

3. Heat the wok without any fat, roast the cumin and dried chillies, stirring continually. Finely grind in a mortar, then mix to a smooth paste with yoghurt, caster sugar and the ginger-onion-juice.

4. Heat oil. Fry cloves, cardamom, cinnamon and bay leaves for 1 minute, don't let them turn brown. Add the remains of the ginger-onion paste and fry for 1 minute, then add the yoghurt mix. Slowly bring to the boil, stirring continually.

5. Give the fish into the wok and leave to simmer over a low heat for approx. 10–15 minutes. Serve with basmati rice.

52

Squid in Chilli Batter

Serves 4

8 medium-sized
squid tubes

Juice of 1 lemon

Salt

200 g/7 oz white bread

3 dried chillies

1 tbsp chilli flakes

2 egg whites

2 1/2 quarts vegetable oil
for deep fat frying

Preparation time

approx. 20 minutes

Per serving

approx. 470 kcal/1 968 kj

39 g P

16 g F

38 g C

1 Thoroughly wash the squid tubes under running water and dry well. Then cut the tubes into wide rings and season with lemon juice and salt. As an alternative, slice open the squid tubes and cut into chunks of 5 cm/2 in.

2 Crumble up the white bread and mix with the finely chopped chillies and the chilli flakes.

3 Whisk the egg whites and dip the squid rings first in egg white, then in the chilli batter. Do this two more times to ensure that the batter will turn out nice and crispy.

4 Deep fat fry the squid rings in the sizzling oil in the wok, divided into several rations, until they are crispy golden. Drain on kitchen paper.

Plaice in a Coconut Coat with Aubergines

Serves 4

1 kg/2 lb 3 oz aubergines

3 tbsp sunflower oil

2 tbsp oyster sauce

1 tbsp fish sauce

300 g/10 oz white bread

5 tbsp desiccated coconut

1 tbsp curry powder

1 tsp turmeric

800 g/1 lb 12 oz plaice fillet

Salt

Flour for the batter

2 egg whites

2 1/2 quarts vegetable oil for deep fat frying

1 tbsp sesame seeds

Preparation time

approx. 30 minutes

Per serving

approx. 725 kcal/3 036 kj

50 g P

32 g F

47 g C

1 Rinse and trim the aubergines and cut into 5 cm/2 in chunks.

2 Stir-fry the aubergines in the wok, in sizzling oil, then season with the oyster and fish sauces. Remove.

3 Crumble up the white bread and mix with desiccated coconut, curry powder and turmeric. Rinse and pat dry the plaice fillet, cut into 4 cm/1.6 in chunks, salt, then dip in the flour, the slightly whisked egg whites and finally in the coconut batter. Repeat this process.

4 Deep fat fry the fish chunks in plenty of sizzling oil in the wok until they are crispy golden. Drain on some kitchen paper. Arrange the fried plaice chunks on the aubergines and sprinkle with sesame seeds.

Scorpionfish with Fried Broccoli and Ginger

Serves 4

4 scorpionfish fillets, with skin

2 tbsp fish sauce

2 green chillies

4 sticks lemon grass

1 leek

500 g/17 oz broccoli

4 tbsp peanut oil

4 tbsp oyster sauce

1 tbsp grated root ginger

Preparation time

approx. 20 minutes

(plus 1 hour
for marinating)

Per serving

approx. 388 kcal/1 634 kj

39 g P

21 g F

5 g C

1 Rinse and pat dry the fish fillets and cut into 2 cm/0.8 in strips. Marinate in the fish sauce and chillies sliced into rings for approx. 1 hour.

2 Cut the lemon grass into 5 cm/2 in sticks. Cut the leek into rings. Rinse the broccoli, break up into florets, peel the stalk and cut into slices.

3 Heat half of the peanut oil in the wok and gently fry the broccoli florets and slices with the lemon grass. Then add the leek rings, pour in the oyster sauce. Towards the end, toss in the grated ginger. Remove and keep warm.

4 Heat the remaining peanut oil in the wok and put in the fish chunks. Carefully fry on all sides over a medium heat, for approx. 5 minutes.

5 Arrange the broccoli and leek on plates and serve one fried fish fillet on each plate.

Salmon with Baby Aubergines and Papaya

Serves 4

500 g/17 oz salmon fillet

1/2 ripe papaya

1/2 green papaya

200 g/7 oz
white baby aubergines

3 coriander leaves

2 tbsp oil

1 tsp curry paste

1 tbsp palm sugar

2 tins coconut milk
(400 ml/14 fl oz each)

2 tbsp fish sauce

4 tbsp oyster sauce

Preparation time

approx. 30 minutes

Per serving

approx. 385 kcal/1 613 kj

28 g P

25 g F

10 g C

1 Rinse and pat dry the salmon fillet and cut into cubes. Peel and seed the papayas and cut into wedges. Rinse the baby aubergines, remove the stalk and cut in halves. Rinse and shake dry the coriander leaves and chop finely.

2 Heat the oil in the wok, fry the curry paste and palm sugar, smoothen with some coconut milk and leave to bubble for a few minutes.

3 Now add the remaining coconut milk, add the aubergine halves and leave to simmer a few minutes more, then season with the fish and oyster sauces.

4 Now add the papaya wedges and let them warm up, then give the salmon strips into the sauce and gently simmer. Stir carefully, making sure that the salmon cooks but does not flake.

5 Towards the end, fold in the coriander leaves and briefly heat up.

Fried Tuna in Spicy Bean Sprout Sauce

Serves 4

1 walnut-sized knob
of fresh root ginger

2 garlic cloves

800 g/1 lb 12 oz
fresh tuna fillet

2 tbsp oyster sauce

2 tbsp fish sauce

2 red chillies

200 g/7 oz
young green beans

4 tbsp sunflower oil

100 g/3.5 oz
bean sprouts

Salt

2 tbsp soy bean paste

Some caster sugar

Preparation time

approx. 25 minutes
(plus 30 minutes
for marinating)

Per serving

approx. 605 kcal/2 535 kj

45 g P

41 g F

5 g C

1 Peel and finely slice the ginger. Peel and finely chop the garlic. Rinse and pat dry the tuna, divide into 4 equal parts, salt lightly and marinate for 30 minutes in some of the oyster and fish sauces, the ginger and garlic.

2 Cut the chillies into rings, rinse and top and tail the beans and cut into 3 cm/ 1.2 in pieces.

3 Briefly stir-fry the tuna on both sides in 2 tablespoons oil in the wok, then remove and keep warm.

4 Heat the remaining oil in the wok and fry the beans with the bean sprouts and the chilli rings. Season with the remaining fish and oyster sauces, the soy bean paste and some sugar. Leave the sauce to thicken a little, then add the tuna and fold in carefully.

Sole with Thai Basil and Kaffir Limes

Serves 4

600 g/1 lb 5 oz sole fillet
400 g/14 oz carrots
2 Kaffir limes
1 tbsp oyster sauce
2 tbsp fish sauce
4 tbsp vegetable oil
3 tbsp soy sauce
1 bunch Thai basil

Preparation time

approx. 15 minutes
(plus 30 minutes
for marinating)

Per serving

approx. 285 kcal/1 195 kj
29 g P
13 g F
10 g C

1. Rinse and thoroughly pat dry the sole and cut into 3 cm/1.2 in strips. Rinse, trim and peel the carrots, halve lengthwise and then cut into diagonal fine slices. Cut the Kaffir limes into fine slices.

2. Marinate the sole strips for 30 minutes in the oyster and fish sauces.

3. Heat the oil in the wok and gently fry the carrot slices. Add the Kaffir lime slices and the fish strips, toss and fry for approx. 2 minutes.

4. Towards the end, pour in the soy sauce and fold in the plucked Thai basil leaves.

Rice Pan with Shiitake Mushrooms Coalfish and Green Chillies

Serves 4

250 g/9 oz
long-grain rice

120 g/2 oz
shiitake mushrooms

2 medium-sized
green chillies

2 shallots

800 g/1 lb 12 oz
coalfish fillet

2 tbsp vegetable oil

4 tsp fish sauce

2 tbsp oyster sauce

125 ml/4.5 fl oz
fish stock

Cayenne pepper

Preparation time

approx. 25 minutes

Per serving

approx. 415 kcal/1 738 kj

41 g P

7 g F

41 g C

1 Cook the long-grain rice according to the instructions on the package and set aside.

2 Trim the shiitake mushrooms and, depending on their size, leave whole, halve or cut into quarters. Peel the shallots and cut into rings. Rinse and pat dry the coalfish and cut into cubes.

3 Heat 1 tablespoon oil in the wok, fry the coalfish until golden brown and remove.

4 Fry the shallots in the remaining oil until transparent, then consecutively add the mushrooms and chillies and season with the fish and oyster sauces. Add the fish stock and leave to simmer gently for 3 minutes.

5 Add the fish and the cooked rice to the vegetables and season to a spicy taste with cayenne pepper.

Coalfish with Baby Aubergines and Red Peppers

Serves 4

600 g/1 lb 5 oz
coalfish fillet

100 ml/3 fl oz rice wine

3 red peppers

200 g/7 oz
baby aubergines

4 tbsp vegetable oil

1 tsp small green chillies

4 tbsp oyster sauce

Preparation time

approx. 15 minutes

(plus 30 minutes
for marinating)

Per serving

approx. 289 kcal/1 212 kj

28 g P

12 g F

5 g C

1 Rinse and pat dry the coalfish fillet and cut into cubes of 3 cm/1.2 in. Pour the rice wine over the fish and marinate for 30 minutes.

2 Rinse and dry the peppers, seed them and cut into 3 cm/1.2 in lozenges. Rinse the aubergines and halve lengthwise.

3 Heat the oil in the wok and stir-fry the aubergines until golden brown. Then add the peppers and chillies and continue frying.

4 Now add the marinated fish cubes and carefully fold in. Towards the end, pour the rice wine marinade and oyster sauce over.

Carp Paddies
with Rice Vinegar Dip

Serves 4

500 g/17 oz carp fillet

Juice of 1 lemon

Salt

1/2 bunch coriander

50 g/1.75 oz ghee

1 tsp grated fresh root ginger

1 red chilli

1/2 tsp five spice powder

1 tbsp fish sauce

4 tbsp vegetable oil

Rice vinegar dip

4 tbsp rice vinegar

1 tbsp caster sugar

2 mild red chillies

Preparation time

approx. 15 minutes

(plus 15 minutes for marinating)

Per serving

approx. 362 kcal/1 514 kj

23 g P

6 g F

5 g C

1. Rinse and pat dry the carp fillet and cut into small cubes. Marinate in the lemon juice and salt and leave in the fridge for 15 minutes. In the meantime, pluck off and mince the coriander leaves.

2. Finely blend the carp cubes in several rations to make a smooth purée. Add the ghee, ginger, finely chopped chilli and coriander and stir until it has become a smooth paste. Season with salt, five spice powder and fish sauce.

3. Wet your hands with water and form the paste into small biscuits, then fry on both sides them in the wok, in sizzling oil, until crispy golden. Leave to drain on kitchen paper.

4. For the dip, chop the mild red chillies and mix with sugar and rice vinegar.

Sweet and Sour Coalfish Chunks in Tandoori Batter

Serves 4

1 pack instant
tempura batter

1 tsp tandoori paste

800 g/1 lb 12 oz
coalfish fillet, salt

2 red and green peppers
each

1 mango

200 g/7 oz Nameko
mushrooms (in a jar)

12 baby sweet corns

2 tbsp caster sugar

5 tbsp rice vinegar

100 ml/3 fl oz
pineapple juice

100 g/3 oz tomato ketchup

1 tsp grated fresh root
ginger

2 tbsp light soy sauce

3 Kaffir lime leaves

2 1/2 quarts sunflower oil
for deep fat frying

3 tbsp sunflower oil
for frying

Preparation time

approx. 35 minutes

Per serving

approx. 705 kcal/2 950 kj

47 g P

19 g F

81 g C

1 Prepare the tempura batter according to the instructions on the package and stir in the tandoori paste. Rinse and pat dry the coalfish fillet, cut into chunks of 3 cm/1.2 in and sprinkle with salt.

2 Rinse, trim and seed the peppers and cut into chunks of 2 cm/0.8 in. Peel the mango and cut into chunks. Drain the Nameko mushrooms and keep the liquid. Diagonally halve the baby sweet corn and briefly stir-fry in the wok, in sizzling oil, with the Nameko mushrooms. Add the peppers and briefly stir-fry. Remove.

3 Caramelise the sugar in the wok until it has turned golden, the pour in the rice vinegar and add the pineapple juice and Nameko liquid. Stir in the ketchup and simmer for 5 minutes. Season with ginger and soy sauce. Add the fried vegetables and the mango chunks.

4 Using a meat fork, dip the fish in the batter and deep fat fry in plenty of sizzling oil for approx. 3 minutes, until crispy golden. Drain on kitchen paper. Mix the fish chunks with the sweet and sour vegetables sauce and garnish with finely chopped Kaffir lime leaves.

72

Cod Curry with Papaya and Fried Cauliflower Florets

Serves 4

600 g/1 lb 5 oz cod fillet

2 tbsp fish sauce

6 tbsp peanut oil

120 g/4 oz
cauliflower florets

100 g/3.5 oz fresh peas

1 tbsp palm sugar

1 tbsp red curry paste

3 tbsp oyster sauce

1 tin unsweetened
coconut milk
(400 ml/14 fl oz)

200 g/7 oz
papaya chunks

Preparation time

approx. 35 minutes

(plus 10 minutes
for marinating)

Per serving

approx. 271 kcal/1 135 kj

30 g P

11 g F

10 g C

1 Rinse and pat dry the cod fillet and cut into strips of 2 cm/0.8 in, then marinate for 10 minutes in the fish sauce.

2 Stir-fry the cauliflower florets in 3 tablespoons oil in the wok for approx. 5 minutes, until golden brown. Then add the fresh peas, stir well and remove.

3 Heat the remaining peanut oil in the wok and dissolve the grated palm sugar. Add the curry paste, fry briefly, then pour in the oyster sauce and 100 ml/3 fl oz water. Leave to thicken slightly, then add the coconut milk.

4 Give the marinated fish strips and papaya chunks into the sauce and leave to simmer for 3 minutes.

5 Towards the end, return the cauliflower florets and peas into the curry and allow to draw a little.

74

Salmon Trout in Hoisin Sauce with Fried Chinese Cabbage

Serves 4

600 g/1 lb 5 oz skinless
salmon trout fillets

1 medium-sized
Chinese cabbage

150 g/5 oz snow peas

4 tbsp vegetable oil

1/2 bunch coriander

1 tsp sambal oelek

3 tbsp hoisin sauce

Preparation time

approx. 20 minutes

Per serving

approx. 315 kcal/1 320 kj

33 g P

15 g F

8 g C

1 Rinse and pat dry the salmon trout fillets and cut into 2 cm/0.8 in chunks. Quarter the Chinese cabbage and chop into pieces of 2 cm/0.8 in. Rinse, dry and slice the snow peas. Rinse and shake dry the coriander and pluck off the leaves.

2 Stir-fry the Chinese cabbage in the wok over a high heat until their edges have turned golden brown and crispy. Remove.

3 Now gently fry the fish chunks in the wok, sprinkled with sliced snow peas, hoisin sauce and sambal oelek. Turn over carefully.

4 Towards the end, return the cabbage, sprinkle with the chopped coriander leaves and toss.

Squid with Garlic and Green Peppercorns

Serves 4

1 kg/2 lb 3 oz squid flesh (not the tentacles and heads)

1 whole garlic bulb

4 tbsp vegetable oil

4 tbsp fish sauce

2 tbsp green pepper-corns

2 tbsp roasted sesame oil

Preparation time

approx. 25 minutes

Per serving

approx. 348 kcal/1 456kj

47 g P

14 g F

2 g C

1 Thoroughly rinse the squid under running water and dry well. Crush the garlic cloves in their skins.

2 Slice open the squid tubes lengthwise and spread out on the work surface, the outside facing down. Make fine rhombus-shaped incisions with the tip of a knife, then cut the squid into chunks of 5 cm/2 in.

3 Heat the sesame and vegetable oils in the wok and fry the crushed garlic cloves.

4 Add the squid chunks, pour in the fish sauce, add the peppercorns and briefly fry.

Recipes with Seafood

Seafood is especially well suited for cooking in the wok. From shrimps to king prawns and scallops to fine lobster, many delicacies from the oceans can be found in Asian cuisine, and they fully unfold their exquisite flavour in the wok.

Venus' Shells
in Coriander Curry Sauce

Serves 4

1.5 kg/3 lb 4 oz
Venus' shells

2 shallots

1 garlic clove

1 bunch coriander

3 tbsp vegetable oil

2 tbsp curry powder

200 ml/7 fl oz
dry white wine

250 g/9 oz single cream

1/2 tsp ginger powder

Preparation time

approx. 25 minutes

Per serving

approx. 524 kcal/2 194 kj

40 g P

32 g F

5 g C

1 Soak the Venus' shells well in water, then rinse under running water and drain. Peel the shallots and cut into rings; peel and finely chop the garlic. Rinse and shake dry the coriander and coarsely chop.

2 Let the oil get very hot in the wok, then add the shallot rings and chopped garlic, sprinkle the curry powder over and briefly fry.

3 Add the drained shells. Pour the white wine over and firmly close the wok.

4 Let the shells open and then remove them from the wok. Now pour the cream into the liquid, season with ginger and reduce to approx. the half.

5 Return the shells to the wok, stir with the sauce and sprinkle with the coarsely chopped coriander.

Spicy Rice Noodles with Shrimps, Lemon Grass and Pineapple

Serves 4

250 g/9 oz rice noodles

1/2 pineapple

2 red chillies

1 bunch spring onions

1 stick lemon grass

2 tbsp vegetable oil

1 tbsp sesame oil

300 g/10 oz shrimps, ready to cook

2 tbsp fish sauce

2 tbsp white rice vinegar

Preparation time

approx. 25 minutes

Per serving

approx. 434 kcal/1 819 kj

25 g P

10 g F

66 g C

1 Briefly cook the rice noodles in boiling water and drain in a colander.

2 Peel the pineapple and cut into small cubes; rinse and dry the chillies and cut into fine rings; rinse and trim the spring onions and also cut into fine rings. Finely chop the lemon grass.

3 Heat the vegetable and sesame oils in the wok, briefly stir-fry the spring onions, add the shrimps, fry, then pour the fish sauce and rice vinegar over.

4 Now add the pineapple cubes and chillies.

5 Towards the end, add the cooked rice noodles, toss well and serve.

Tiger Prawns with Rice Wine and Oyster Sauce

Serves 4

20 large tiger prawns with shell and head

200 ml/7 fl oz rice wine

6 tbsp vegetable oil

1 tsp palm sugar

4 tbsp oyster sauce

1 tsp chilli flakes

Preparation time

approx. 15 minutes

(plus 30 minutes
for marinating)

Per serving

approx. 305 kcal/1 276 kj

19 g P

17 g F

3 g C

1 Thoroughly rinse the tiger prawns under running water, dry well and marinate for 30 minutes in the rice wine.

2 Heat the oil in the wok, dissolve the grated palm sugar, stir in the oyster sauce, add the chilli flakes and then stir-fry the tiger prawns on all sides, over a very high heat.

3 Pour the marinade over, firmly close the wok and leave the tiger prawns to simmer for approx. 3–5 minutes.

4 Remove the tiger prawns from the wok and serve sprinkled with the sauce.

Fried Scallops with Young White Cabbage

Serves 4

20 g/scant 1 oz
dried black fungi

1 medium-sized young
white cabbage

6 tbsp sunflower oil

1 tbsp oyster sauce

2 tbsp fish sauce

8 scallops without roe

1 tbsp flour

1 tbsp light soy sauce

2 tbsp hoisin sauce

Some caster sugar

Preparation time

approx. 30 minutes

(plus 1 hour for soaking)

Per serving

approx. 301 kcal/1 258 kj

20 g P

15 g F

19 g C

1 Soak the black fungi in cold water for 1 hour. Halve the young white cabbage, remove the stalk and cut the leaves into fine slices.

2 Heat 4 tablespoons oil in the wok and stir-fry one third of the cabbage, then season with some of the oyster, fish and light soy sauces. Repeat this process until all the cabbage has been fried. Remove and keep warm.

3 Drain the black fungi, trim and chop them. Halve the scallops. Coat each half in some flour and fry in the wok in the remaining, sizzling oil on both sides until crispy golden.

4 Briefly stir-fry the black fungi, then carefully fold in with the scallops and cabbage. Towards the end, season to taste with soy sauce, hoisin sauce and sugar.

Clams with Fried Noodles

Serves 4

200 g/7 oz
vermicelli glass noodles

3 tbsp oil

200 g/7 oz leek

1 tbsp peanut oil

15 water chestnuts
(in a jar)

Salt

Caster sugar

1 tsp glutamate

1/2 l/17 fl oz
chicken stock

1 small tin bamboo
shoots (sliced)

1 tin clams (380 g/13 oz)

2 tbsp cornflour

Preparation time

approx. 40 minutes

Per serving

approx. 218 kcal/911 kj

13 g P

9 g F

10 g G

1 Cook the vermicelli according to the instructions on the package in boiling water.

2 Remove, drain and fry in sizzling oil. Keep warm.

3 Trim, rinse and finely slice the leek.

4 Heat the peanut oil in the wok and fry the leek. Drain the water chestnuts and add to the wok. Add the spices and stir-fry for approx. 3 minutes.

5 Pour the chicken stock in and bring to the boil.

6 Drain the bamboo shoots and clams and add to the wok.

7 Dissolve the cornflour in 3 tablespoons water and pour into the wok, leave to simmer for approx. 3 minutes.

8 Serve the clams with the fried noodles.

Shrimps with Galangal and Chillies

Serves 4

600 g/1 lb 5 oz
shrimps (frozen)

1 pack medium-sized,
mild green chillies

2 tbsp vegetable oil

1 tsp grated galangal
root

1 tsp tom yum goong
paste

200 ml/7 fl oz
chicken stock

Preparation time

approx. 20 minutes

Per serving

approx. 196 kcal/821 kj

28 g P

7 g F

1 g C

1 Slowly thaw the shrimps – this is best done in the fridge.

2 Rinse, dry and trim the chillies and halve lengthwise. Heat the oil in the wok and fry the chillies until they turn soft.

3 Add the thawed shrimps, mix with galangal and tom yum goong paste and then pour in the chicken stock.

4 Cook the shrimps until the liquid has evaporated.

Mixed Seafood
in Ginger Stock

Serves 4

6 tbsp fish sauce

2 large knobs of ginger

1 bunch coriander

1 courgette

1 large leek

1 carrot

1 Kaffir lime

100 g/3.5 oz
shiitake mushrooms

200 g/7 oz shrimps

12 prawns

4 crabs

400 g/14 oz
white fish in chunks

Some chilli oil

Preparation time

approx. 25 minutes

Per serving

approx. 310 kcal/1 299 kj

46 g P

7 g F

12 g C

1 Simmer 3 l/3 quarts water with the fish sauce and the sliced but not peeled ginger for 10 minutes, then pour through a sieve. Rinse and shake dry the coriander and pluck off the leaves.

2 Rinse the courgette, leek and carrot, dry, trim and slice them. Halve the Kaffir lime. Trim the shiitake mushrooms and finely slice.

3 Wash and thoroughly pat dry the shrimps, prawns, crabs and fish chunks.

4 Put the seafood and vegetables into the wok and pour the ginger stock over them, bring to the boil and leave to simmer gently for 5 minutes. Sprinkle with coriander leaves and chilli oil.

Fried Wan Tan Filled with Cream Cheese and Shrimps

Serves 4

200 g/7 oz
cocktail shrimps

1 bunch chives

200 g/7 oz cream cheese
(whole fat)

Juice of 1 lemon

2 tbsp rice vinegar

1 pinch grated fresh root
ginger

1/2 tsp five spice powder

Salt

16 wan tan leaves (frozen)

2 egg whites

4 tbsp sesame seeds

2 1/2 quarts vegetable oil
for deep fat frying

Preparation time

approx. 25 minutes

Per serving

approx. 450 kcal/1 883 kj

22 g P

31 g F

19 g C

1 Thoroughly rinse the shrimps under running water, dry well and chop coarsely. Rinse and shake dry the chives and finely chop.

2 Mix the cream cheese, shrimps and chives. Season to taste with lemon juice, rice vinegar, ginger, five spice powder and salt.

3 Spread out the wan tan leaves, put 1 teaspoon of the cheese spread into the middle of each leaf. Coat the edges with egg white and flap the leaves over diagonally to form little triangular packs.

4 Coat the wan tans with the remaining egg white, then sprinkle with sesame seeds and deep fat fry in plenty of sizzling oil until crispy golden. Drain on kitchen paper.

Stir-Fried Wok Scallops

Serves 4

250 g/9 oz
Chinese egg noodles

2 tbsp oil

100 g/3.5 oz
crab meat (in a tin)

Pepper

2 tbsp soy sauce

1 tbsp cornflour

1 tbsp sesame oil, salt

3 spring onions

1 knob root ginger
(3 cm/1.2 in)

500 g/17 oz
scallops, shelled

3 tbsp peanut oil

1 tbsp sake

For the sauce

2 tbsp soy sauce

1 tsp cornflour

salt, caster sugar

Preparation time

approx. 35 minutes

Per serving

approx. 515 kcal/2 156 kj

26 g P

17 g F

51 g C

1 Cook the noodles in plenty of boiling water for approx. 5 minutes. Drain and keep warm.

2 Heat the oil in the wok and fry the crab meat with some pepper.

3 Stir the soy sauce with cornflour, 250 ml/ 9 fl oz water, the sesame oil and some salt. Pour over the crab meat and bring to the boil, stirring continually. Mix the sauce with the noodles and keep warm.

4 Trim, rinse and coarsely chop the spring onions. Peel and chop the ginger. Rinse the scallops, drain and halve if required.

5 Heat the peanut oil in the wok over a very high heat and stir-fry the spring onions and ginger. Add the scallops and sake and stir-fry for 2 minutes.

6 Mix the soy sauce with the cornflour, 4 tablespoons water, salt and sugar and pour over the scallops. Cook for approx. 1 minute, stirring all the time.

7 Mix the scallops with the noodles and serve.

Lobster with Pineapple in Tamarind Sauce

Serves 4

2 lobsters
(500 g/17 oz each)

1/2 pineapple

4 tbsp vegetable oil

1 tbsp palm sugar

1 tbsp tamarind sauce

2 tbsp oyster sauce

4 tbsp fish sauce

2 tins coconut milk
(400 ml/14 fl oz each)

5 Kaffir lime leaves

Preparation time

approx. 20 minutes

Per serving

approx. 467 kcal/1 957 kj

42 g P

16 g F

34 g C

1 Rinse the lobster, cut open, remove the innards and pound the claws.

2 Peel the pineapple and cut into bite-sized chunks.

3 Stir-fry the lobster pieces in the wok over a very high heat, add the pineapple, sprinkle with finely chopped palm sugar, then pour the tamarind, fish and oyster sauces over. Add the coconut milk and leave to simmer for approx. 5 minutes.

4 Towards the end, stir in the finely chopped Kaffir lime leaves.

Fried Rice with Seafood

Serves 4

250 g/9 oz
long-grain rice

4 mild, medium large
green chillies

4 tbsp vegetable oil

400 g/14 oz mixed
seafood, ready to cook

100 g/3.5 oz
young green peas

200 g/7 oz
fresh bean sprouts

4 tbsp fish sauce

2 tbsp oyster sauce

1 tsp chilli garlic sauce

Preparation time

approx. 30 minutes

Per serving

approx. 365 kcal/1 530 kj

23 g P

14 g F

35 g C

1 Cook the rice according to the instructions on the package and set aside. Rinse, trim and seed the chillies and cut into rings.

2 Heat the vegetable oil in the wok and briefly stir-fry the seafood.

3 Add the peas and bean sprouts, then toss in the cooked rice.

4 Season with the fish, oyster and chilli garlic sauces. Towards the end, stir in the chopped chillies.

5 Should the rice start to stick to the rim of the wok, add a little water.

Serves 4

1 kg/2 lb 3 oz
large mussels
2 tbsp chilli oil
10 shallots
1 whole garlic bulb
4 tbsp vegetable oil
1 tbsp nam prik
2 tbsp fish sauce

Preparation time

approx. 25 minutes

Per serving

approx. 344 kcal/1 441 kj
30 g P
20 g F
9 g C

1 Thoroughly wash the mussels under running water, remove the hairs. Heat the chilli oil in the wok, add the mussels and let them open.

2 Remove the mussels, open them up and discard the empty shell halves.

3 Peel the shallots and cut into fine rings; peel and finely slice the garlic. Slowly fry in the remaining oil until they have turned crispy.

4 Stir in the nam prik, return the mussels, pour the fish sauce over and toss. Serve the mussels on plates and sprinkle them with the cooking liquid.

Chinese Egg Noodles with Broccoli and Red Onions

Serves 4

250 g/9 oz
Chinese egg noodles

400 g/14 oz
broccoli florets

3 red onions

6 tbsp vegetable oil

4 tbsp fish sauce

4 tbsp sweet and sour
sauce

2 tbsp dried shrimps

Preparation time

approx. 25 minutes

Per serving

approx. 639 kcal/2 676 kj

6 g P

19 g F

93 g C

1 Cook the noodles, drain, run under cold water and set aside.

2 Rinse and dry the broccoli florets. Peel and halve the onions and cut into strips of 2 cm/0.8 in.

3 Heat half the oil in the wok, stir-fry the broccoli florets and then remove. Fry the onions in the remaining oil until they have turned transparent.

4 Return the broccoli, pour the fish sauce over and season with the sweet and sour sauce. Toss in the cooked egg noodles and heat up. Towards the end, stir in the dried shrimps.

Rock Lobster
in Aromatic Thai Sauce

Serves 4

32 medium-sized
rock lobsters

4 tbsp vegetable oil

1 tsp tom yum goong
paste

1 tsp nam prik

1 tbsp oyster sauce

250 ml/9 fl oz fish or
chicken stock

Some rau om leaves

Preparation time

approx. 25 minutes

Per serving

approx. 324 kcal/1 357 kj

43 g P

13 g F

3 g C

1 Rinse and pat dry the rock lobsters, remove the heads, lightly crush the tails and claws.

2 Heat the oil in the wok and stir-fry the rock lobsters on all sides.

3 Add the tom yum goong paste, nam prik and oyster sauce, pour in the fish or chicken stock and cover; leave to simmer gently for approx. 10 minutes.

4 Towards the end, remove the lid, let the sauce thicken a little more and season with rau om.

Fried Prawns with Soy Sauce and Lemon Grass

Serves 4

20 fresh whole prawns

1/2 bunch coriander

1 small garlic clove

1 stick lemon grass

1 thumb-sized knob root ginger

1/2 tsp curry powder

5 tbsp peanut oil

2 tbsp soy sauce

50 ml/2 fl oz water or fish stock

Preparation time

approx. 15 minutes

(plus 2 hours
for marinating)

Per serving

approx. 317 kcal/1 326 kj

38 g P

15 g F

2 g C

1. Rinse the prawns under running water and dry on kitchen paper. Place into a porcelain dish. Rinse and shake dry the coriander and pluck off the leaves.

2. Peel and finely chop the garlic, cut the lemon grass into rings, peel and grate the root ginger. In a bowl, whisk together with curry, 3 tablespoons peanut oil and soy sauce and then pour over the prawns. Cover with cling film and leave to marinate in the fridge for approx. 2 hours.

3. Remove the prawns from the marinade, heat the remaining peanut oil in the wok and stir-fry the prawns on both sides for approx. 2 minutes.

4. Towards the end, pour in the marinade and fish stock or water and stir. Serve garnished with coarsely chopped coriander leaves.

Yellow Coconut Rice with Shrimps

Serves 4

250 g/9 oz rice

1 tbsp turmeric

1 bunch spring onions

1/2 bunch coriander

250 g/9 oz
skinned shrimps

2 tbsp desiccated
coconut

4 tbsp vegetable oil

Some salt

Preparation time

approx. 30 minutes

Per serving

approx. 355 kcal/1 485 kj

16 g P

16 g F

34 g C

1 Cook the rice with the turmeric, which will give it a nice yellow colour.

2 Trim, rinse and dry the spring onions and cut into rings. Rinse and shake dry the coriander and pluck off the leaves.

3 Heat the oil in the wok and fry the spring onion rings with the shrimps, season with salt.

4 Add the cooked rice, sprinkle with desiccated coconut, toss and fry until the rice is hot.

5 Sprinkle with the coriander leaves and serve.

King Prawns and Tofu from the Wok

Serves 4

300 g/10 oz king prawns
300 g/10 oz tofu
1 bunch spring onions
3 tbsp sesame oil
3 tbsp oyster sauce
2 tbsp soy sauce
2 tsp cornflour
1/2 tsp caster sugar

Preparation time

approx. 40 minutes

Per serving

approx. 215 kcal/1 050 kj
23 g P
13 g F
9 g C

1 Remove the shells of the king prawns, make an incision into their back and remove the bowels, then rinse and pat dry thoroughly.

2 Cut the tofu into large cubes.

3 Trim and rinse the spring onions and cut into strips.

4 Heat the oil and stir-fry the king prawns with the tofu and spring onions for approx. 5 minutes.

5 Mix the oyster sauce with soy sauce, cornflour, sugar and 3 tablespoons water.

6 Add the sauce to the prawns, bring to the boil and leave to simmer until it thickens. Remove, arrange on plates and serve.

Fried Egg Noodles
with Shrimps and Snow Peas

Serves 4

250 g/9 oz
Chinese egg noodles

300 g/10 oz snow peas

1 bunch spring onions

2 small, mild green
chillies

2 tbsp sesame oil

250 g/7 oz
cocktail shrimps

2 tbsp light soy sauce

2 tbsp sweet and sour
chilli sauce

6 eggs

Salt

Preparation time

approx. 35 minutes

Per serving

approx. 562 kcal/2 355 kj

29 g P

19 g F

56 g C

1 Cook the egg noodles in salted water according to the instructions on the package. Top and tail the snow peas, rinse, dry and halve diagonally. Rinse and trim the spring onions and cut into thin, diagonal rings. Rinse and dry the chillies and cut into fine strips.

2 Heat the sesame oil in the wok and stir-fry the spring onions. Add first the snow peas, then the chilli strips. Towards the end, toss in the egg noodles and fry for 3 minutes more.

3 Add the shrimps and season with the soy and chilli sauces. Push the noodle mixture up towards the rim of the wok and pour the whisked eggs into the centre. Leave to settle a bit, then stir and mix with the fried noodles.

Tiger Prawns in Chilli Batter

Serves 4

1 pack instant
tempura batter

1 tbsp chilli flakes

1 tbsp paprika powder

20 large, whole
tiger prawns

2 1/2 quarts vegetable oil
for deep fat frying

2 lemons

Kaffir lime leaves

Preparation time

approx. 25 minutes

Per serving

approx. 437 kcal/1 831 kj

22 g P

14 g F

52 g C

1 Prepare the tempura batter according to the instructions on the package, stir in the chilli flakes and paprika and set aside.

2 Thoroughly rinse the prawns under running water and dry. Now cut off the legs and beard with kitchen scissors, remove the tail shell, leaving the tip of the tail.

3 Heat the oil in the wok to 160 °C/320 °F. Bathe the prawns in the batter and deep fat fry in the sizzling oil for 5 minutes, until crispy golden. Drain on kitchen paper.

4 Arrange the tiger prawns on plates, sprinkle with lemon juice and serve garnished with Kaffir lime leaves.

Steamed Rice Balls Filled with Shrimps

Serves 4

200 g/7 os basmati rice

200 g/7 oz shelled shrimps

2 tbsp fish sauce

1/2 tsp grated root ginger

1 tsp chilli flakes

6 tbsp fish sauce

Juice of 1 lime

3 red chillies

1 tbsp minced coriander

Preparation time

approx. 35 minutes

Per serving

approx. 174 kcal/729 kj

13 g P

3 g F

24 g C

1. Cook the basmati rice according to the instructions on the package and leave to cool.

2. For the filling, mix the shrimps with the fish sauce and grated ginger.

3. Wet your hands, then form the rice into little balls. Press a hole into the centre with your finger, fill in the shrimps paste and close again. Proceeding like this, make 12 balls all in all.

4. Place the balls into bamboo baskets and sprinkle with chilli flakes. Pour some water into the wok and bring to the boil, then place the baskets inside, one on top of the other, and firmly close the wok.

5. After 15 minutes, swap the baskets, exchanging the top basket with the bottom one. Steam for 30 minutes altogether. For the dip, whisk fish sauce with lime juice, finely chopped chillies and coriander.

Crabs with Curry Sauce and Coriander

Serves 4

12 crabs

4 tbsp vegetable oil

1 tbsp yellow curry paste

1 tbsp palm sugar

4 tbsp oyster sauce

2 tbsp fish sauce

2 tins coconut milk
(400 ml/14 fl oz each)

5 coriander leaves

1 tbsp desiccated
coconut

Preparation time

approx. 20 minutes

Per serving

approx. 232 kcal/970 kj

17 g P

15 g F

7 g C

1 Thoroughly rinse the crabs under running water, dry well and then cut in halves.

2 Heat the oil in the wok and stir-fry the crabs. Then add the curry paste, finely chopped palm sugar, the oyster and fish sauces and fry some more.

3 Pour in the coconut milk and bring to the boil; leave to simmer until the crabs have turned bright red.

4 Add the finely chopped coriander leaves to the sauce and serve sprinkled with desiccated coconut.

Fried Scallops
with Spring Onions

Serves 4

12 shelled scallops, without roe

1 pinch grated lemon zest

1 tbsp roasted sesame oil

1 bunch spring onions

200 g/7 oz tomatoes

1 garlic clove

1 red chilli

4 tbsp sunflower oil

1 tsp freshly grated root ginger

2 tbsp oyster sauce

2 tbsp fish sauce

Preparation time

approx. 35 minutes

(plus 10 minutes
for marinating)

Per serving

approx. 142 kcal/593 kj

12 g P

8 g F

4 g C

1. Thoroughly rinse the scallops under running water, dry well and marinate in the lemon zest and sesame oil for 10 minutes.

2. Rinse and trim the spring onions and cut diagonally into 4 cm/1.2 in sticks. Briefly dip the tomatoes in boiling water, rinse under cold water and skin. Then cut them in quarters, remove the seeds, and cut into wedges. Finely chop the peeled garlic and seeded chilli.

3. Stir-fry the spring onions in half of the oil in the wok, then add tomatoes, ginger, garlic and chilli and fry 3 minutes more. Season to taste with the oyster and fish sauces. Remove.

4. Heat the remaining oil in the wok and fry the scallops until golden brown. Serve arranged with the vegetables.

Tiger Prawns with Sweet Chilli Sauce and Limes

Serves 4

20 tiger prawns,
with shells and heads

2 limes

6 tbsp vegetable oil

1 tbsp roasted
sesame oil

2 tbsp fish sauce

150 ml/5 fl oz
sweet chilli sauce

Preparation time

approx. 10 minutes

Per serving

approx. 296 kcal/1 242 kj

19 g P

19 g F

8 g C

1 Thoroughly rinse the tiger prawns under running water and dry well. Slice the limes.

2 Heat the vegetable and sesame oils in the wok and fry the prawns on all sides over a high heat.

3 After having turned the prawns over for the first time, add the sliced limes and continue frying for 3 minutes more.

4 Add the fish and chilli sauces. Continue stir-frying until the sauce has coated the prawns on all sides.

Index of Recipes